Literature Res
Forms

MW01691313

Grades 1-3

Written by Staci Marck
Illustrated by Peggy Collins and S&S Learning Materials

ISBN 1-55035-743-3

Revised January 2006
 "We acknowledge the financial support of the Government of Canada through the Book Publishing Industry Development Program (BPIDP) for this project."

Published in the United States by:
On the Mark Press
3909 Witmer Road PMB 175
Niagara Falls, New York
14305
www.onthemarkpress.com

Published in Canada by:
S&S Learning Materials
15 Dairy Avenue
Napanee, Ontario
K7R 1M4
www.sslearning.com

At A Glance™

Learning Expectations	Vocabulary Development	Sequencing & Summarizing	Character Analysis	Creative Thinking	Synthesis & Evaluation
Vocabulary, Word Use & Conventions					
• Identify parts of speech - nouns, verbs and adjectives	•				
• Identify/recognize alliteration, rhyming words, consonant blends, compound words, contractions	•				
• Use connecting words (first, then, next, after, last) to retell a story		•			
• Use a dictionary to expand vocabulary	•				
Reasoning & Critical Thinking					
• Organize information	•	•	•	•	
• Sequence and summarize story elements, recall details		•		•	•
• Identify main idea, provide supporting evidence		•			•
• Identify and describe character traits, and cite supporting evidence			•		
• Identify and describe similarities and differences			•		•
• Make connections between the story and personal experiences/the real world			•	•	•
• Make inferences based on personal interpretation of the story			•	•	•
• Make predictions about the story				•	•
• Analyze and evaluate story elements				•	•
• Develop opinions and express personal point of view		•		•	•
• Distinguish between fact and fiction using evidence from the text					•
• Create media texts - comic strip, advertisement		•			•
• Creative writing - sequel to the story, join the story, rewrite the ending				•	•
• Forms of writing - letter from a character, book review			•		•
• Follow instructions to make artwork	•			•	
• Express own interpretation of a story through visual and performing arts (illustrations, puppet and puppet show, character mask and play, book award, book cover, bookmark)	•	•	•	•	•
• Develop interviewing skills - interview the author, a character					•

Literature Response Forms

Table of Contents

Teacher Assessment Rubric

Student's Name: ______________________

Put a check mark in the box that indicates the student's level of achievement.

Level 1 - requires assistance, inconsistent effort, shows limited understanding of concepts
Level 2 - requires minimal assistance, shows limited understanding of concepts
Level 3 - independent, consistent effort, shows general understanding of concepts
Level 4 - independent, consistent effort, shows thorough understanding of concepts

Criteria	Level 1	Level 2	Level 3	Level 4
Vocabulary Development				
• Understands the text at a word level.				
• Uses knowledge of language structures and word categories.				
Sequencing and Summarizing Events				
• Retells a story in proper sequence and recalls details.				
• Identifies and describes some story elements.				
Character Analysis				
• Demonstrates an understanding of character traits.				
• Uses knowledge of character to evaluate roles and cites supporting details.				
Creative Thinking				
• Makes connections between the story and the real world.				
• Demonstrates an understanding of the story through artistic interpretation.				
Synthesis and Evaluation				
• Expresses thoughts, feelings and opinions about a story.				
• Evaluates story elements and conclusion/resolution.				
• Draws conclusions and makes generalizations based on his/her personal interpretation of the story.				

Comments: ____

____

____

Student Self-Assessment Rubric

Name: ______________________________ Date: ______________

Put a check mark in the box that best describes you.

	Needs Improvement ☆	Sometimes ☆☆	Almost Always ☆☆☆	Always ☆☆☆☆
✔ I am a good listener.				
✔ I remained on task.				
✔ I was prepared and organized.				
✔ I used all the resources available.				
✔ I made connections to the world.				
✔ I reviewed my work for corrections.				
✔ My work is neat and colored.				
✔ I know what I am good at.				
✔ I know what I need to work on.				
✔ I know when I need to ask for help.				

Answer each question with a complete sentence.

1. What did you enjoy learning about the most? ______________________

____

2. What would you like to learn more about? ______________________

____

3. What can you improve upon in your work? ______________________

____

Literature Response Forms

Planning and Implementation

1. **Why Use Literature Response Forms?**

   - Reading comprehension is the process in which a reader builds meaning from a text and his/her prior knowledge. It involves thinking before, during, and after the reading process. Assessment of reading comprehension can only be done indirectly because it is a thought process.
   - Literature response forms help you assess if your students understand the texts they are reading, as they encourage students to make creative connections between the text and their previous learning, thereby strengthening their understanding.
   - Literature response forms are engaging, purposeful activities that students can complete on their own, which opens up classroom time for you to conduct guided reading lessons in small groups, or conference with individual students. Instruction is scaffolded so that once students have practiced filling out the forms, they can complete them independently.

2. **Introducing Literature Response Forms in a Mini-Lesson**

   - Literature response forms should be introduced as a whole class mini-lesson after a shared reading. Choose a book that supports the skill focus of the literature response form that you wish to introduce.
   - Explicitly teach your students the skill focus of the response form using an enlarged copy of the work sheet on an overhead, the chalkboard, or chart paper, so that all of the students can easily see the template. Explain the concepts being introduced. Use a "think aloud" strategy to model your thinking as you complete the form so that the students can see the process you go through to respond. Engage the students in a guided practice process by asking them questions, encouraging discussion, and listing a variety of their responses which highlight the range of possibilities of appropriate responses.
   - After the mini-lesson, give the students their own copy of the form to complete. Let them practice the form to ensure mastery by the majority of students before introducing a new work sheet.
   - Use this mini-lesson format to introduce each new literature response form.
   - Introduce the response forms in an order that best meets your students' learning needs and grade level. You may wish to present several work sheets from one category to emphasize a single skill area, or one form from each category to emphasize different skill areas.
   - Once several response forms have been explicitly taught and modeled, and the students have had sufficient practice working with them, they can be used as independent literature responses for shared, guided, or independent reading comprehension assessment.

3. **Selecting Literature Response Forms for Your Classroom**

   - Introduce enough forms to give students a choice of follow-ups to shared, guided, or independent reading (for example, a mimimum of three).
   - Make copies of the forms, place them in a folder, and allow students to select the response they wish to complete. Alternatively, you may choose to assign specific forms to individuals or small groups for practice in a particular skill area.
   - Continue to introduce new literature response forms so that students maintain their motivation. Vary the response activities to allow students to develop, practice, and master a variety of skills.

Literature Response Forms

4. Sharing Time

- Allow time for students to share their responses so that they may celebrate their accomplishments. Sharing helps to develop a community of learners as students gather new ideas from peers, and fosters self-confidence in individual students as they learn to discuss their responses.
- Sharing can be done weekly, as a whole class, through individual assignment on particular days, or daily within guided reading groups.

5. Helping Students Choose Books

- **Shared reading** or **read aloud** texts can be at any reading level because the teacher is reading the text to the class and modeling the process.
- **Guided reading** texts should be chosen so that the students within the group can read it with 90 to 94 percent accuracy and comprehension. The text is slightly harder than those they can read independently because students will receive scaffolded teacher support during the lesson.
- **Independent reading** texts should be at the student's "just right" level – a book which can be read at greater than 95 percent accuracy by the student independently. If the student makes more than five reading errors on the first page, then the text is too difficult.

6. Tips for Organizing Your Classroom Library

- **Shared reading** and **read aloud** texts should be kept in a separate location prior to introducing them to the class. This will help to keep them unique and engaging for the majority of the students because they will be unfamiliar. Many of these selections will be beyond the students' independent reading level anyway, and therefore inaccessible to them. After you have read a text to them, make it available to students for independent reading. Students love to retell stories that they are familiar with.
- **Guided reading** texts should also be kept in a separate location prior to introducing them to the class, since they are instructional texts. Guided reading texts should be new to students so that you are able to help them build their reading strategies, comprehension, and fluency. These texts are meant to be just slightly above the students' independent reading level. Once introduced, they can be kept in reading group baskets with a different basket for each guided reading group. In each basket, students may use gift bags or small covered boxes about the size of granola bar boxes, to house their individual guided reading texts. Four to six previously read guided reading texts can be used as warm up books before the new guided reading text is introduced during the lesson to help build fluency.
- **Independent reading** texts can be organized in many different ways. If students are grouped in small groups within the classroom, small plastic bins can be used to correspond to the number of tables within the classroom. Place a variety of books from all different levels in the bins - include picture books, magazines, newspaper articles, pamphlets, etc. Authentic reading materials at a variety of levels should be available to the students. Keep the rest of your books in a place that is inaccessible to students so that after the bins have been rotated between the groups, you will have new material to put in each bin. For instance, if you have five groups in the classroom, you will need five bins. Color code or number the bins, and rotate them over five weeks between the groups. By the end of the fifth week, each table has seen each bin. Then exchange the reading materials.

7. Tracking and Assessment

- The **reading log** (p. 13) and **tracking sheet** (p. 14) should be completed by each student independently, and are useful tools for monitoring students' activities and preferences at a glance, such as the number and type of completed work sheets, and fiction versus nonfiction reading rate.

Literature Response Forms

- The **teacher's assessment rubric** (p. 4) will help you gather information on students' strengths and needs, and should be used to direct independent instruction and mini-lessons. It may also be used to provide feedback to students and guide them in setting personal learning goals.
- The **student self-assessment rubric** (p. 5) should be explained and modeled so that students may evaluate their own thinking and learning.
- One-to-one **teacher-student conferences** should be approximately five minutes long. During these sessions, students benefit from feedback on their progress and the teacher benefits from the opportunity to meet with students individually to gather performance-based assessment information. You may follow the format on the conference form provided (p. 11) to bring meaningful structure to these sessions.

8. Using the Blank Forms

- In order to meet the unique needs of your classroom, you may wish to use the blank forms (p. 78) to create additional activities or tracking sheets that correspond with the work sheets introduced.

Modeling the Literature Response Activities

In this section you will find suggestions for modeling the five different types of response forms. One example is given for each of the skill categories. The first one, using the Verb Action work sheet as an example for the vocabulary development activities, is described in detail from start to finish of the mini-lesson. You may adapt this modeling format, as needed, to introduce each literature response form in this resource. Be sure to read "Introducing Literature Response Forms in a Mini-Lesson" (p. 6) prior to reading the modeling suggestions below.

Vocabulary Development

These work sheets focus on the analysis of language conventions used in a story. As students build their understanding of vocabulary and language structures, they develop a deeper understanding of the story itself.

Example: Verb Action (p. 17)

- Begin the mini-lesson by explaining to the students the focus of the lesson (learning to identify verbs). Tell the students that verbs are action words, such as "talk", "yell", "cry", and so on.
- Introduce the book and the main character. Ask the students to listen for verbs that describe actions of the main character in the story, as you read it aloud. Then begin reading.
- Stop midway through the story to check for understanding. Have the students name some verbs that the main character has done in the story so far. Record them on the enlarged copy of the response form that you have displayed at the front of the class before continuing the reading.
- Repeat the same procedure once you have finished the story. Ask the students to make a sentence using one of the verbs from the list. Record the sentence on the form, and repeat this process two more times. Have the students identify the verb in each sentence, and underline it on the form. Ask them to confirm whether or not the underlined words are verbs, based on the definition you provided.
- Provide each student with their own copy of the literature response form that you have just modeled, and let them practice completing it on their own with either the story you have just read, or independent story selections. Check for understanding and mastery before giving it to students to complete during Reader's Workshop.

Literature Response Forms

Sequencing and Summarizing Events

These work sheets focus on reviewing the elements of a story. Story elements include the setting, characters, problem, events, and solution/resolution of the story. The 5W questions (Who, What, Where, When, and Why) are often used in conjunction with How to prompt the retell of the story. Readers are challenged to retell the story in the sequence it occurred in the book. Each story element is a crucial component to the story, so every element must be remembered during the retell on the response activity.

Example: Story Map (p. 33)

- Tell the students that they will be learning how to retell a story by describing the setting, main characters, problem, events, and how the problem is solved. Define each of these elements (i.e., the setting is the location and the time in which the story takes place).
- Introduce the book and remind the students to focus, as you read, on identifying where and when it takes place, who the main characters are, and what the main problem in the story is.
- Begin reading, and stop midway through the section to check for understanding. Ask the students to tell you one element that they have heard described so far. Record a few responses on the form, and continue this questioning until they have given you the setting, main characters and problem. Then begin reading again.
- Repeat the same procedure once you have finished reading the story, this time focusing on events and the story's resolution. Record a few of the students' examples. Then ask them to confirm whether or not their responses describe the setting, characters, and other elements based on the definitions you provided.

Character Analysis

These work sheets focus the students' attention on the characters in the book, what they are like, how they live, and the ways they solve problems. Readers are challenged to identify similarities and differences between themselves and the characters, and between the characters and people they know. Characters are frequently the most memorable part of a story to children. Analyzing the behaviors of these characters helps bring them to life, and engages students in such thought provoking questions as "What would this character be like if he or she lived in my city, or even next door?"

Example: Character Clues (p. 50)

- Start the mini-lesson by telling the students that they will be looking for clues in the story that tell what the main character is like. Explain that these clues may be words or phrases that tell how the character acts or behaves, looks, feels, and things that he or she says.
- Introduce the book and identify the main character that they will be studying. Remind the students to listen for character clues as you read the story.
- Begin reading, and stop midway through the section to check for understanding. Have the students recall some of the clues they have heard about so far. Record a few responses on the form before continuing the reading.
- Repeat the same procedure when you have finished reading the section. Record a few of the students' examples. Be sure to give examples of the kinds of answers you are looking for.

Literature Response Forms

Creative Thinking

These exercises focus on the development of students' creative abilities in order to enhance their understanding of the story. Students are required to reflect on, and in some cases modify, the story using their own ideas and imagination. Readers are challenged to bring new life to the story by adding new characters or joining the story. They may also make the story more real in their imagination by creating a character puppet or book award, etc.

Example: Picture Perfect (p. 57)

- Begin the mini-lesson by telling the students that they will be exploring how they can show their feelings about a story through art. Give some examples of words that describe feelings, and ask the students what kinds of stories might make a person feel these ways. Demonstrate how they might express one of these feelings in a picture.
- Introduce the book and tell the students to notice how they are feeling about the story as you read.
- Begin reading the text, and stop midway through the section to check for understanding. Have the students name some feelings they have experienced so far, and explain what about the story made them feel that way. Record a few of the students' responses on the chalkboard. Ask them what kind of picture they would draw to show this feeling, and make a sketch of it. Then continue the reading.
- Repeat the same procedure once you have finished reading the book. Add a few more examples from students to the list.

Synthesis and Evaluation

In this section, students synthesize and evaluate information from the story by relating it to their own life experiences. Readers are challenged to develop personal opinions regarding favorite elements, most important character, overall quality of the book (would they recommend it to a friend?), etc., as well as interact with characters or the author through interviews. By applying their knowledge of the story in these ways, they may develop a more advanced level of comprehension and demonstrate higher order thinking skills.

Example: Book Reviewer Report (p. 66)

- At the start of the mini-lesson, explain that they will be learning how to review a book in order to persuade others to read it or not read it. In order to review a book, they must tell what it is about and explain what they like and do not like about it.
- Before reading, tell the students to listen for details in the story that tell whether the book is fiction (made up) or nonfiction (true or factual), and think about what they like or do not like about the story.
- Begin reading, and stop midway through to check for understanding. Ask the students if they think the book is fiction or nonfiction and why. Record some examples.
- Complete the reading, and ask the students to describe what the book is about. Ask specific questions if necessary to draw out the important information. Ask them what part of the story they liked the most, and record their answers. Then ask how many stars they would award the book (five stars is the best), and why. Record a few of their answers.
- Then ask if they liked the book enough to recommend it to a friend, and why they think this. Remind them that their answers should be persuasive enough that their friends will want to follow their recommendations. Be sure to give examples of the kinds of answers you are looking for.

Literature Response Conference Form

Student's Name: ______________________ **Date:** ____________

Title: ______________________ **Level:** ____________

Record of Student's Retelling:

- Begins retelling with title and author of the book. Yes ☐ No ☐
- Retells story with beginning, middle, and end. Yes ☐ No ☐

Comments: ____

____

- Identifies setting, time and place. Yes ☐ No ☐
- Names main character. Yes ☐ No ☐
- Mentions other characters. Yes ☐ No ☐
- Uses story vocabulary in the retelling. Yes ☐ No ☐
- Identifies main idea. Yes ☐ No ☐

Comments: ____

____

- Identifies supporting details in sequential order. Yes ☐ No ☐

Comments: ____

____

- Makes inferences. Yes ☐ No ☐

Comments: ____

____

- Makes connections with the text. Yes ☐ No ☐

Comments: ____

____

Literature Response Forms

List of Work Sheets

Vocabulary Development
1. Vocabulary Scramble
2. Noun Search
3. Verb Action
4. Describing Words
5. Dictionary Development
6. Word Triangles
7. Create a Word Search
8. Alliteration Exploration
9. Rhyming Rhythms
10. Blend Bugs
11. Put It Together
12. Contraction Hunt

Sequencing and Summarizing Events
1. Story Train
2. First, Then, Next, Last
3. Story Scoop
4. Story Path
5. Story Steps
6. Story Board
7. Story Map
8. Cartoon Strip
9. Main Idea
10. Circle Story Map
11. Book Sharing
12. 5W Map

Character Analysis
1. Character Web
2. Same and Different
3. Character Comparisons
4. Who Am I?
5. You've Got Mail!
6. Prince or Princess Charming
7. Missing Person
8. A New Friend
9. Character Hunt
10. Make a Wish
11. Feelings
12. Character Clues

Creative Thinking Activities
1. Create a Puppet
2. Book Award
3. Retell Chain
4. Character Mask
5. Then What Happened?
6. Design a Cover
7. Picture Perfect
8. Bookmark
9. Add a Character
10. Join the Story
11. Poster Power
12. Memory Stone
13. Looking into Pictures
14. Make a Connection
15. Star Story

Synthesis and Evaluation
1. Book Reviewer Report
2. Book Talk
3. Tell a Friend
4. Analyzer
5. Character Critic
6. Problem Solver
7. Climbing Climax
8. List the Facts
9. Interview an Author
10. Character Chat
11. Book Buddy
12. It All Changed

Literature Response Forms

______________'s Reading Log

Date	Title	Author	F	NF

Color the square in the **F** column **BLUE** if you read a **Fiction** (made up) book. **Color** the square in the **NF** column **RED** if you read a **Nonfiction** (true or factual) book. Try to have an equal number of blue and red squares.

Literature Response Tracking Sheet

Name: ______________________

Color the box of each completed activity.

Vocabulary Development

❑ 1. Vocabulary Scramble	❑ 2. Noun Search	❑ 3. Verb Action
❑ 4. Describing Words	❑ 5. Dictionary Development	❑ 6. Word Triangles
❑ 7. Create a Word Search	❑ 8. Alliteration Exploration	❑ 9. Rhyming Rhythms
❑ 10. Blend Bugs	❑ 11. Put It Together	❑ 12. Contraction Hunt

Sequencing and Summarizing Events

❑ 1. Story Train	❑ 2. First, Then, Next, Last	❑ 3. Story Scoop
❑ 4. Story Path	❑ 5. Story Steps	❑ 6. Story Board
❑ 7. Story Map	❑ 8. Cartoon Strip	❑ 9. Main Idea
❑ 10. Circle Story Map	❑ 11. Book Sharing	❑ 12. 5W Map

Character Analysis

❑ 1. Character Web	❑ 2. Same and Different	❑ 3. Character Comparisons
❑ 4. Who Am I?	❑ 5. You've Got Mail!	❑ 6. Prince or Princess Charming
❑ 7. Missing Person	❑ 8. A New Friend	❑ 9. Character Hunt
❑ 10. Make a Wish	❑ 11. Feelings	❑ 12. Character Clues

Creative Thinking Activities

❑ 1. Create a Puppet	❑ 2. Book Award	❑ 3. Retell Chain
❑ 4. Character Mask	❑ 5. Then What Happened?	❑ 6. Design a Cover
❑ 7. Picture Perfect	❑ 8. Bookmark	❑ 9. Add a Character
❑ 10. Join the Story	❑ 11. Poster Power	❑ 12. Memory Stone
❑ 13. Looking into Pictures	❑ 14. Make a Connection	❑ 15. Star Story

Synthesis and Evaluation

❑ 1. Book Reviewer Report	❑ 2. Book Talk	❑ 3. Tell a Friend
❑ 4. Analyzer	❑ 5. Character Critic	❑ 6. Problem Solver
❑ 7. Climbing Climax	❑ 8. List the Facts	❑ 9. Interview an Author
❑ 10. Character Chat	❑ 11. Book Buddy	❑ 12. It All Changed

Name: ____________________
Date: ____________________
Title: ____________________
Author: ____________________

Vocabulary Scramble

- Find **eight** interesting words from your story. Print them in the **My Words** column.
- **Scramble** the words by mixing the letters (**example: school - olsoch**). Write each scrambled word in the **Scrambled Words** column.
- Have someone **unscramble** the words under the heading **Answers**. Fold the paper so the My Words column is hidden before sharing!

	My Words	Scrambled Words	Answers
1			
2			
3			
4			
5			
6			
7			
8			

Vocabulary Development #1

Name:	______________________
Date:	______________________
Title:	______________________
Author:	______________________

Noun Search

Nouns are the **people**, **animals**, **places** or **things** in a story. Find the nouns in your book and print them in the columns.

Example: **Franklin Goes To School**

People & Animals	Places	Things
Franklin	school	shoes
mother	home	zippers

People & Animals	Places	Things

Vocabulary Development #2

Name: ____________________
Date: ____________________
Title: ____________________
Author: ____________________

Verb Action

Verbs are **action words.** Here are some action words you may find:

talk yell cry sing eat drink

Write six verbs or action words that the main character did in the story.

____________ ____________ ____________

____________ ____________ ____________

Write three sentences using three different action words from the story. Make the sentences tell a story about the main character and what he or she did. **Underline** each action word you used.

1. ____

____

2. ____

____

3. ____

____

Vocabulary Development #3

Name: ______________________
Date: ______________________
Title: ______________________
Author: ______________________

Describing Words

Describing words, or **adjectives**, give detail to a story. (**Example: how big – large, enormous**). Find words in the story that describe:

- how high ______________________
- how low ______________________
- how fast ______________________
- how slow ______________________
- how big ______________________
- how small ______________________
- how long ______________________
- how short ______________________

Write two sentences of your own using two different adjectives. Underline the describing word in the sentence. (**Example: Franklin's dog was large.**)

1. ______________________

____

2. ______________________

____

Vocabulary Development #4

Name: ______________________

Date: ______________________

Title: ______________________

Author: ______________________

Dictionary Development

Find **five** words in the story that you find interesting, confusing, or difficult to understand. In the **first column**, write the page number where you found the word. In the **second column**, write the word. In the **third column**, tell what you think the word means. Then, look it up in the dictionary. In the **last column**, tell what the word really means.

Example:

Page	Word	I think it means...	Now I know it means...
2	command	To tell someone to do something.	To control or order someone to do a task.

Page	Word	I think it means...	Now I know it means...

Vocabulary Development #5

Name: ______________________

Date: ______________________

Title: ______________________

Author: ______________________

Word Triangles

Choose **three** words from your story. Start with the first letter of one word. Add a letter on each line below it. Build your word, letter by letter, until it is complete.

Example:

p
pe
pen
penc
penci
pencil

Vocabulary Development #6

Name: ____________________

Date: ____________________

Title: ____________________

Author: ____________________

Create a Word Search

Find **nine** words from your story that you think are interesting. List each word at the bottom of the page. Put the words on the grid **horizontally** (—), **vertically** (|), or **diagonally** (/, \). Then, fill in the rest of the squares with letters. See if a friend can find your hidden words by circling them on the grid.

Words to find:

______________ ______________ ______________

______________ ______________ ______________

______________ ______________ ______________

Vocabulary Development #7

Name: ____________________

Date: ____________________

Title: ____________________

Author: ____________________

Alliteration Exploration

Alliteration is the use of words with the same initial letter or sound. Choose **three** different sounds, then find **all** the words from your story that share that same beginning letter or sound.

Write a silly sentence using all the words that start with the same sound.

Example: Sound __b__ - broke baby balloon Bob

Baby Bob's balloon broke.

Sound ______

Words ____________ ____________ ____________ ____________

____

____

Sound ______

Words ____________ ____________ ____________ ____________

____

____

Sound ______

Words ____________ ____________ ____________ ____________

____

____

Vocabulary Development #8

Name: ______________________
Date: ______________________
Title: ______________________
Author: ______________________

Rhyming Rhythms

Rhyming words have similar sound patterns. (**Example: sheep, keep, beep**). Look in your story for rhyming words. Find **five** rhyming pairs.

Print the rhyming words. **Draw** a picture of each pair.

Rhyming Word Pairs

1. ____________ ____________

2. ____________ ____________

3. ____________ ____________

4. ____________ ____________

5. ____________ ____________

Vocabulary Development #9

Name: ____________________

Date: ____________________

Title: ____________________

Author: ____________________

Blend Bugs

A **consonant blend** is two different consonants that make a new sound when put together.

Example: bl br cl cr dr fl fr gl gr pl pr scr sl sm sn sp spl spr st str sw

Choose **six** consonant blends from the box above. Print them across the top of the table. **Find and print** words from your story that begin with each consonant blend.

str						
string						
straw						
strong						
stripe						
strap						
strain						
strawberry						

On a piece of construction paper, create **blend bugs**. Put the consonant blend in the head, and the rest of each word in a part of the body. **Draw** your blend bug starting with the head so that the word can be read.

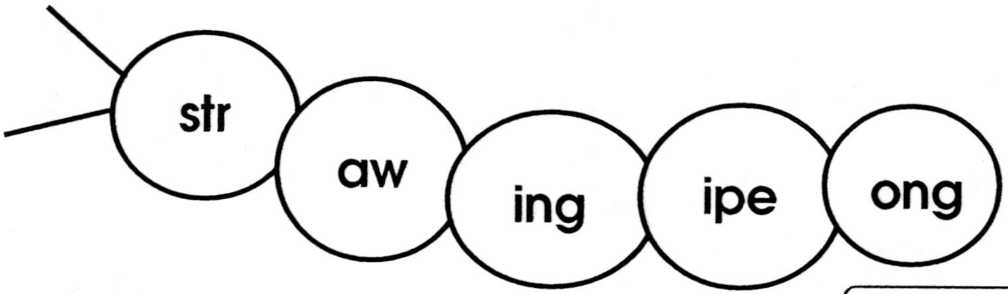

Vocabulary Development #10

Name: ____________________
Date: ____________________
Title: ____________________
Author: ____________________

Put It Together

Compound words are two words joined together that make a new word. The two words by themselves mean different things than the compound word.

Find two compound words from your story. **Draw** a picture of each word on its own, then draw what the new word looks like as a compound word.

Example: base + ball = baseball

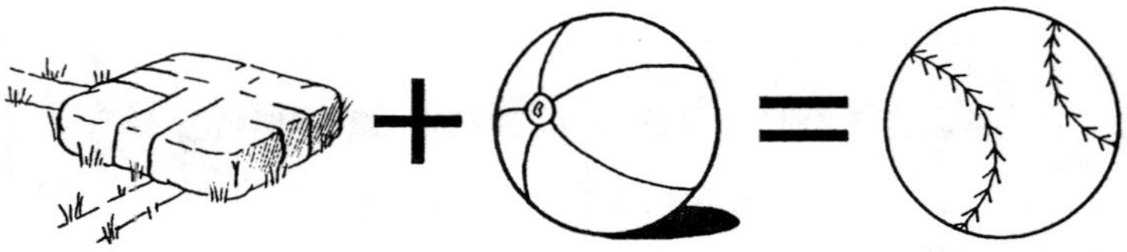

Compound Words

_________ + _________ = ______________

_________ + _________ = ______________

Vocabulary Development #11

Name: ______________________
Date: ______________________
Title: ______________________
Author: ______________________

Contraction Hunt

Contractions are formed when two words are joined together with an apostrophe, and part of the second word is left off. This is often done with a pronoun (a word used in place of a noun, example: he, she, I, they) and a verb, or with a verb and the word "not".

Hunt for contractions in your book. List all of the contractions that you can find, and print the two words that form each contraction. Record the missing letters.

Example: I'm = I am = missing a   **didn't = did not = missing o**

1. ____________ = ____________ ____________ = missing ______
2. ____________ = ____________ ____________ = missing ______
3. ____________ = ____________ ____________ = missing ______
4. ____________ = ____________ ____________ = missing ______
5. ____________ = ____________ ____________ = missing ______
6. ____________ = ____________ ____________ = missing ______
7. ____________ = ____________ ____________ = missing ______
8. ____________ = ____________ ____________ = missing ______
9. ____________ = ____________ ____________ = missing ______
10. ____________ = ____________ ____________ = missing ______

Vocabulary Development #12

Name: ______________________
Date: ______________________
Title: ______________________
Author: ______________________

Story Train

Make a summary of your story in the chart.

Print what happened in the **beginning**, **middle**, and **end** of the story.

Draw a picture at the bottom illustrating each part of the story.

Beginning	Middle	End

Sequencing and Summarizing Events #1

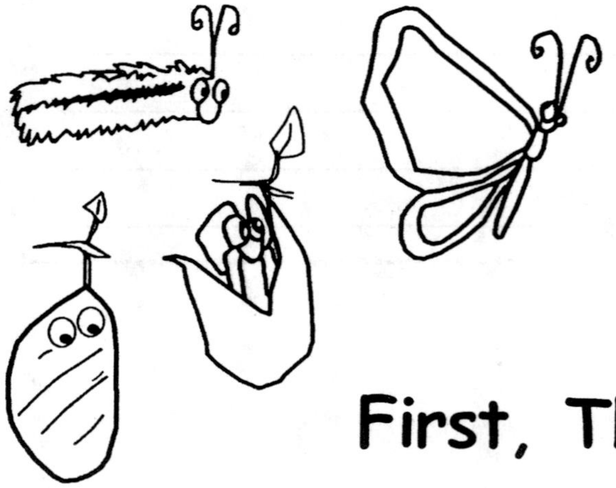

Name: ______________________
Date: ______________________
Title: ______________________
Author: ______________________

First, Then, Next, Last

Complete each section below to summarize the main events of your story.

First: ____

____

____

____

Then: ____

____

____

____

Next: ____

____

____

____

Last: ____

____

____

____

Sequencing and Summarizing Events #2

Name: ____________________
Date: ____________________
Title: ____________________
Author: ____________________

Story Scoop

Make a **summary** of your story in the ice cream scoops. Cut out the pieces and create an ice cream cone. Display your scoop on the story for your friends to see.

In the beginning ______

Next ______

Then ______

In the end ______

Sequencing and Summarizing Events #3

Name: ______________________

Date: ______________________

Title: ______________________

Author: ______________________

Story Path

Use the organizer to summarize the events of your story in the order in which they happened. **Draw** a picture of the story in the center.

1. Who was in the story?

____

____

____

2. Where did it take place?

____

____

____

3. When did it happen?

____

____

____

4. The story started when

____

____

____

5. In the middle

____

____

____

6. The story ended when

____

____

____

Sequencing and Summarizing Events #4

Name: ______________________

Date: ______________________

Title: ______________________

Author: ______________________

Story Steps

Follow the arrows to retell the events of the story in the order in which they happened.

Setting

____
____
____
____
____

→

Story Introduction

____
____
____
____
____

→

Main Characters

____
____
____
____
____

↓

The Problem or Main Goal

____
____
____
____

←

Main Event #1

____
____
____
____
____

↓

Main Event #2

____
____
____
____
____

→

Main Event #3

____
____
____
____
____

→

Resolution

____
____
____
____
____

Name:	______________
Date:	______________
Title:	______________
Author:	______________

Story Board

Complete the chart to retell your story.

Where and when does the story take place? (Setting)	Who is in the story? (Characters)	What happens in the story? (Plot)	How does the the story end? (Conclusion)
Where		Actions/Events	
When			

Sequencing and Summarizing Events #6

Name: ______________________

Date: ______________________

Title: ______________________

Author: ______________________

Story Map

Use your book to help retell the story.

Setting: 

____

____

Main Characters: 

____

____

Problem: 

____

____

Event 1: ______________________________________

____

Event 2: ______________________________________

____

Event 3: ______________________________________

____

Problem Solved/Goal Achieved: 

____

____

Draw a picture of your favorite part of the story on a separate sheet of paper.

Name: ______________________

Date: ______________________

Title: ______________________

Author: ______________________

Cartoon Strip

Make a cartoon strip to retell your story.

Draw a picture in each box. **Print** a sentence in each bubble to explain what is happening in the square. One event should follow another as it happened in the story. Remember to start with the first event, and end with the last event.

Sequencing and Summarizing Events #8

Name: ______________________

Date: ______________________

Title: ______________________

Author: ______________________

Main Idea

What is the book about? Print the main idea of the book in the first box.

Example: This story is about a girl who moved to Chicago.

Fill in the other boxes, describing what happened in the book, in the order the events occurred.

What is the book about?

What happened in the book?

What is the most important event or idea that happened in the book?

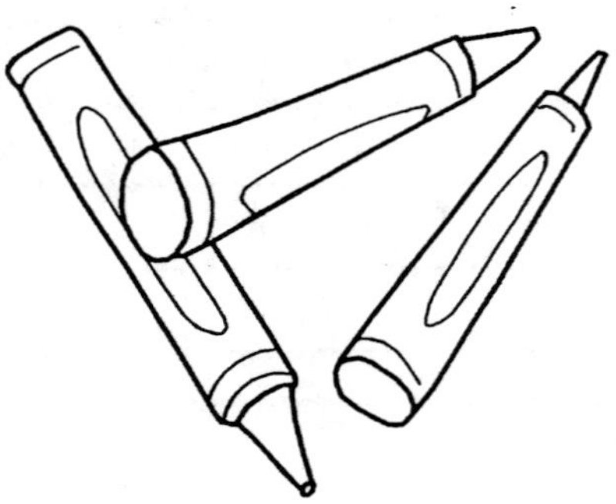

Name: ______________________
Date: ______________________
Title: ______________________
Author: ______________________

Circle Story Map

Complete the circle story map with details about the characters, setting, problem, and solution of the story. In the center, draw a picture of your favorite part of the story.

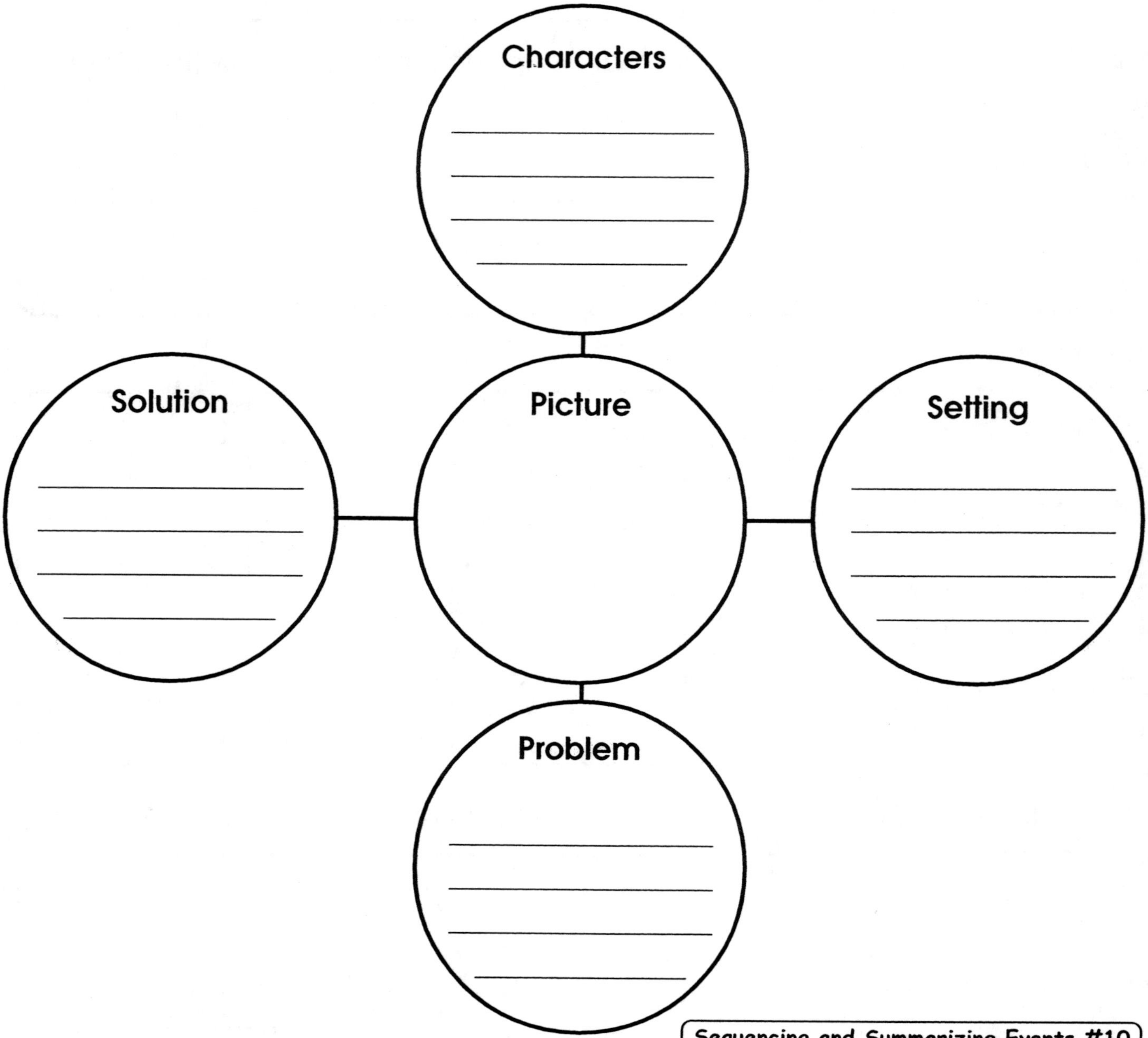

Name:	______________________
Date:	______________________
Title:	______________________
Author:	______________________

Book Sharing

Share your thoughts about your book with a friend by answering the **5 W's**.

Who is the book about? ______________________

____

What happened in the book? ______________________

____

Where did it take place? ______________________

____

When did it take place? ______________________

____

Why did it take place? ______________________

____

How did it happen? ______________________

____

Would you recommend this book to a friend? ❐ Yes ❐ No

Why or why not? ______________________

____

____

Name: ______________________

Date: ______________________

Title: ______________________

Author: ______________________

5W Map

Most stories tell **who**, **what**, **when**, **where**, **why** and **how**. **Who** tells the names of the characters in the story. **What** tells the main events in the story. **When** tells the time in which the story happened. **Where** tells the location of the story. **Why** tells the reasons events happened as they did, and explains characters actions. **How** explains the actions the characters used to make the events happen. Fill in the boxes with details from your book.

What?

____

____

____

____

____

When?

____

____

____

____

____

Where?

____

____

____

____

____

Who?

____

____

____

____

____

Why?

____

____

____

____

____

____

How?

____

____

____

____

____

____

Sequencing and Summarizing Events #12

Name: ____________________

Date: ____________________

Title: ____________________

Author: ____________________

Character Web

On the web, list character traits of the main character in your story. What is he or she like? How does he or she act? How does he or she think and feel? Include the page number where the character trait was seen in the story.

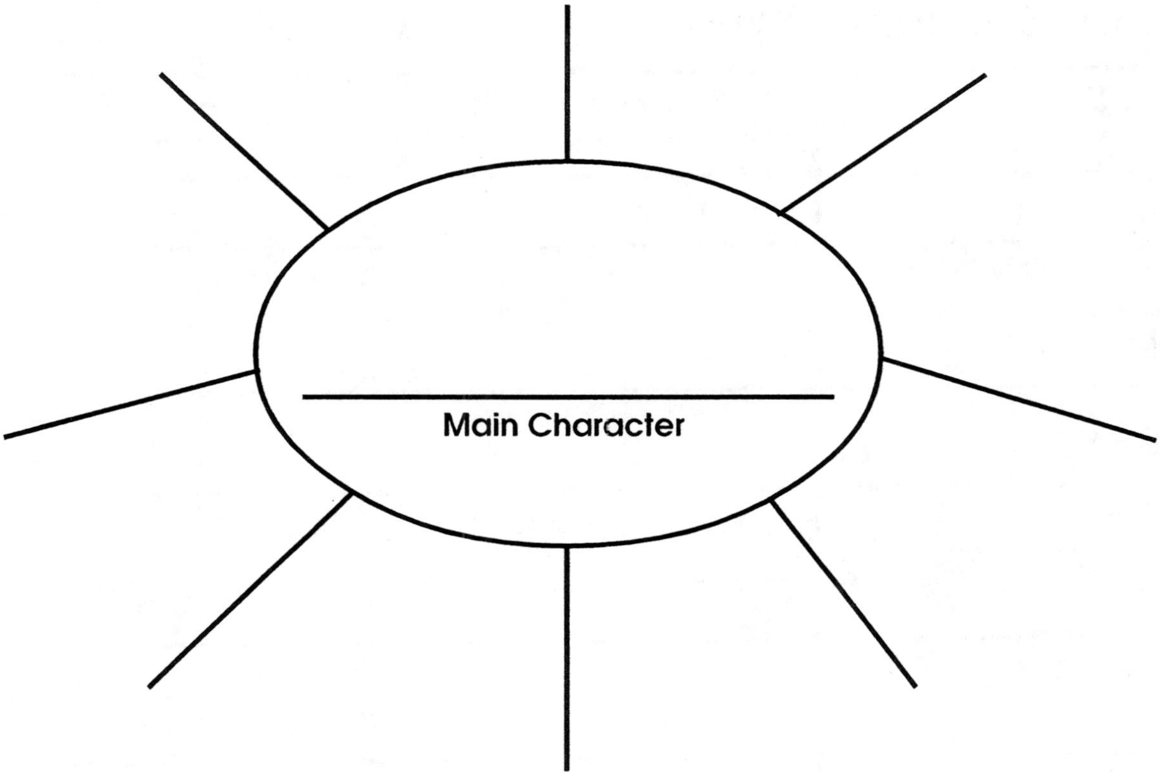

Example:

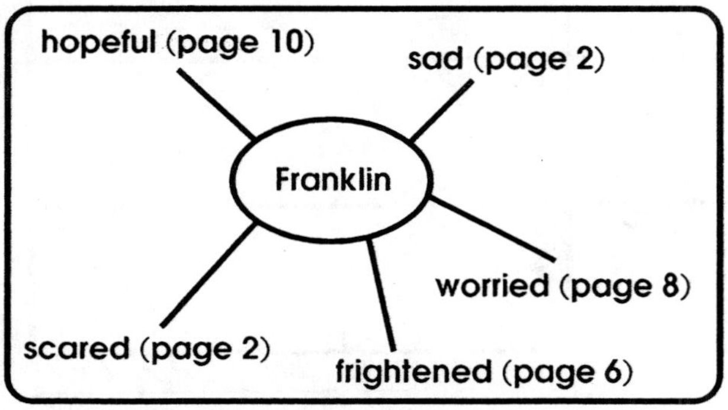

Character Analysis #1

Name:	______________________
Date:	______________________
Title:	______________________
Author:	______________________

Same and Different

How are fictional characters' lives different from real life? In the chart below, give features of your life and features of a character's life from your story. In the middle column, list features that are the same in both your life and the character's life.

For example, using the Mary-Kate and Ashley Mystery Series novels…

In my life…	In both my life and the characters' life…	In the story…
	we have friends.	
I do not have a twin, but I have sisters that I fight with all the time.		Mary-Kate and Ashley are twin sisters and they never fight.

Fill in the chart below.

In my life...	In both my life and ______________________'s life...	In the story...

Character Analysis #2

Name: ____________________
Date: ____________________
Title: ____________________
Author: ____________________

Character Comparisons

Character traits tell how someone **looks**, **feels**, **thinks** and **acts**. (**Example: hopeful, resourceful, clever**).

Compare one of the characters in your story to yourself.

List the character traits that are individual or unique to each of you in the outer circles. In the middle area, list the character traits that you share.

My unique character traits	Character traits that ____________ and I share.	____________'s unique character traits

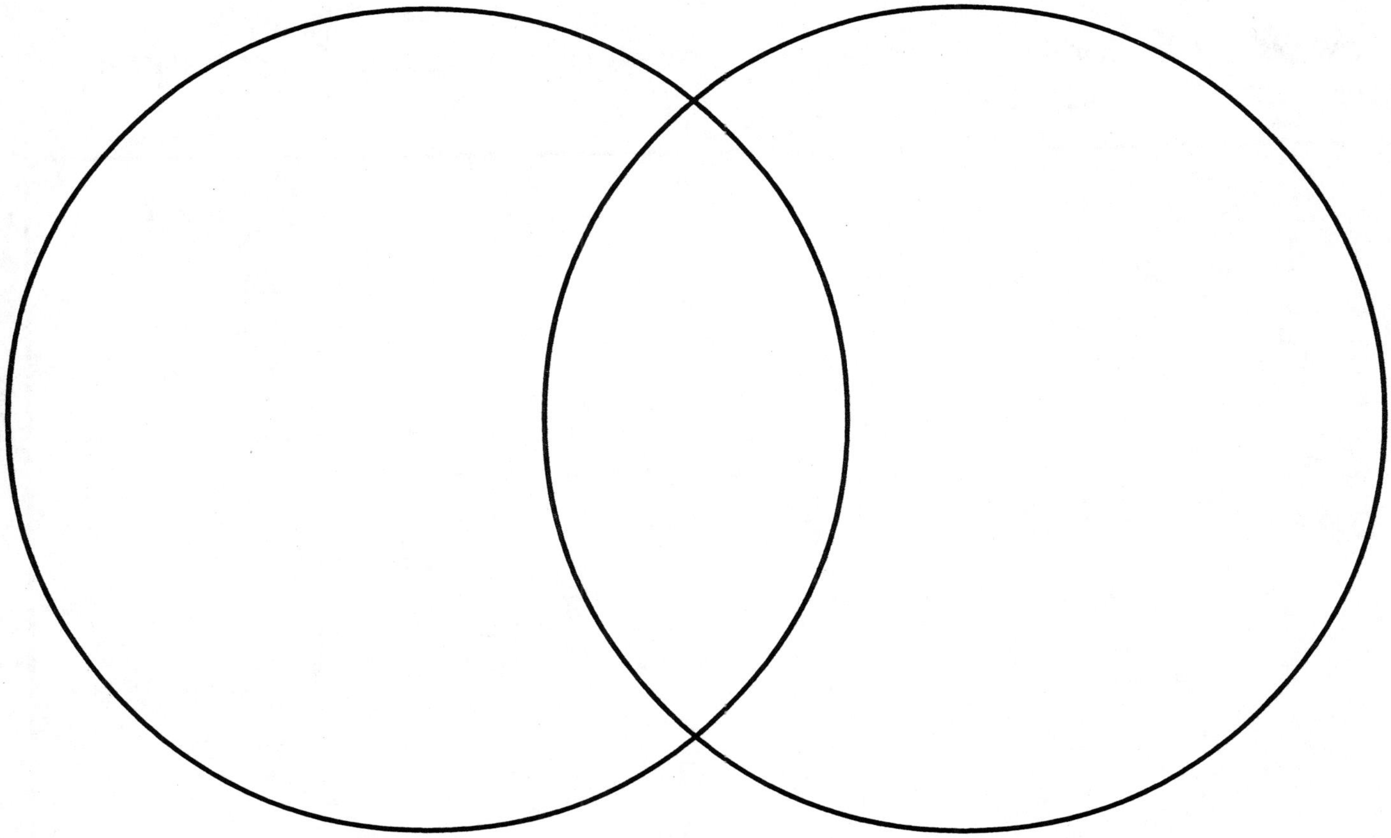

Character Analysis #3

Name: ____________________
Date: ____________________
Title: ____________________
Author: ____________________

Who Am I?

Select a character from your story to draw. What makes the character special? What does he or she look like? What does he or she do and say?

Write five clues that would help a friend guess who the character is.

1. ______________________________
2. ______________________________
3. ______________________________
4. ______________________________
5. ______________________________

Draw his or her portrait. **Cut** it up into a three-piece puzzle. Ask a friend to guess who the character is.

Character Analysis #4

Name: ______________________

Date: ______________________

Title: ______________________

Author: ______________________

You've Got Mail!

You have received a letter from a character in your story. This character tells you about him or herself, and asks about your favorite activities and hobbies. Print the letter below. Remember to sign the letter with the character's name, and address it to yourself!

Dear ______________________ ,

____

____

____

____

____

____

____

____

____

____

____

Yours truly,

____

Character Analysis #5

Name: ______________________
Date: ______________________
Title: ______________________
Author: ______________________

Prince or Princess Charming

In the fairy tale Cinderella, Prince Charming is very **pleasing** in his thoughts, feelings, and actions.

Who is **charming** in your story? How does he or she show it? Describe how this character is charming, and give examples from the story.

______________________ **is very charming.**

Character Analysis #6

Name: ____________________
Date: ____________________
Title: ____________________
Author: ____________________

Missing Person

Help! A character from your story is missing or lost.

Give the police a description of your character so they can find him or her. Include as much information as you can. Be sure to draw a picture to help them find the character.

Missing!

Name: ____________________

Hair color: ____________________

Eye color: ____________________

Lives at: ____________________

____

Last seen wearing: ____________________

____

Last seen at: ____________________

____

If seen call: ____________________

Character Analysis #7

Name: ______________________

Date: ______________________

Title: ______________________

Author: ______________________

A New Friend

A character from your story has moved in next door to you. You become best friends. Tell what you like best about your new friendship.

______________________ **is my friend.**

____

____

____

____

____

____

____

____

____

____

____

____

____

Draw a picture on the back of this page of you and your friend playing together.

Character Analysis #8

Name: ______________________
Date: ______________________
Title: ______________________
Author: ______________________

Character Hunt

Find five pictures or objects that tell something about a character from your story. Put the objects in a paper bag. Ask a friend to guess who the character is.

Write out how each object or picture reminds you of the character. **(Example: Object - paint brush, Clue - Junie B. Jones likes to paint pictures at school.)**

Character Hunt Clues

1. Object - ______________________

Clue - ______________________

2. Object - ______________________

Clue - ______________________

3. Object - ______________________

Clue - ______________________

4. Object - ______________________

Clue - ______________________

5. Object - ______________________

Clue - ______________________

Character Analysis #9

Name: ______________________

Date: ______________________

Title: ______________________

Author: ______________________

Make a Wish

Imagine you are a character from the story. **Write** about what you would do and how you would feel as this character. **Draw** a picture of your new self.

Character Analysis #10

Name: ______________________
Date: ______________________
Title: ______________________
Author: ______________________

Feelings

Choose a character from your story.

In the box beside each of the feelings, describe a time in the story when the character felt that way.

List the page number where you found the example.

Character: ______________________

Feeling	Example from the story	Page
happy		
angry		
sad		
excited		
embarrassed		
afraid		

Did your character experience another emotion in the story? Describe it...

____

____

____

Character Analysis #11

Name: ____________________

Date: ____________________

Title: ____________________

Author: ____________________

Character Clues

The author of your story gives lots of clues throughout the story about what the main character is like. Fill in the blanks with sentences or short phrases which tell how the main character acts, looks, feels, and what he or she says. (**Example: Franklin feels worried about starting school. He looks like a turtle.**)

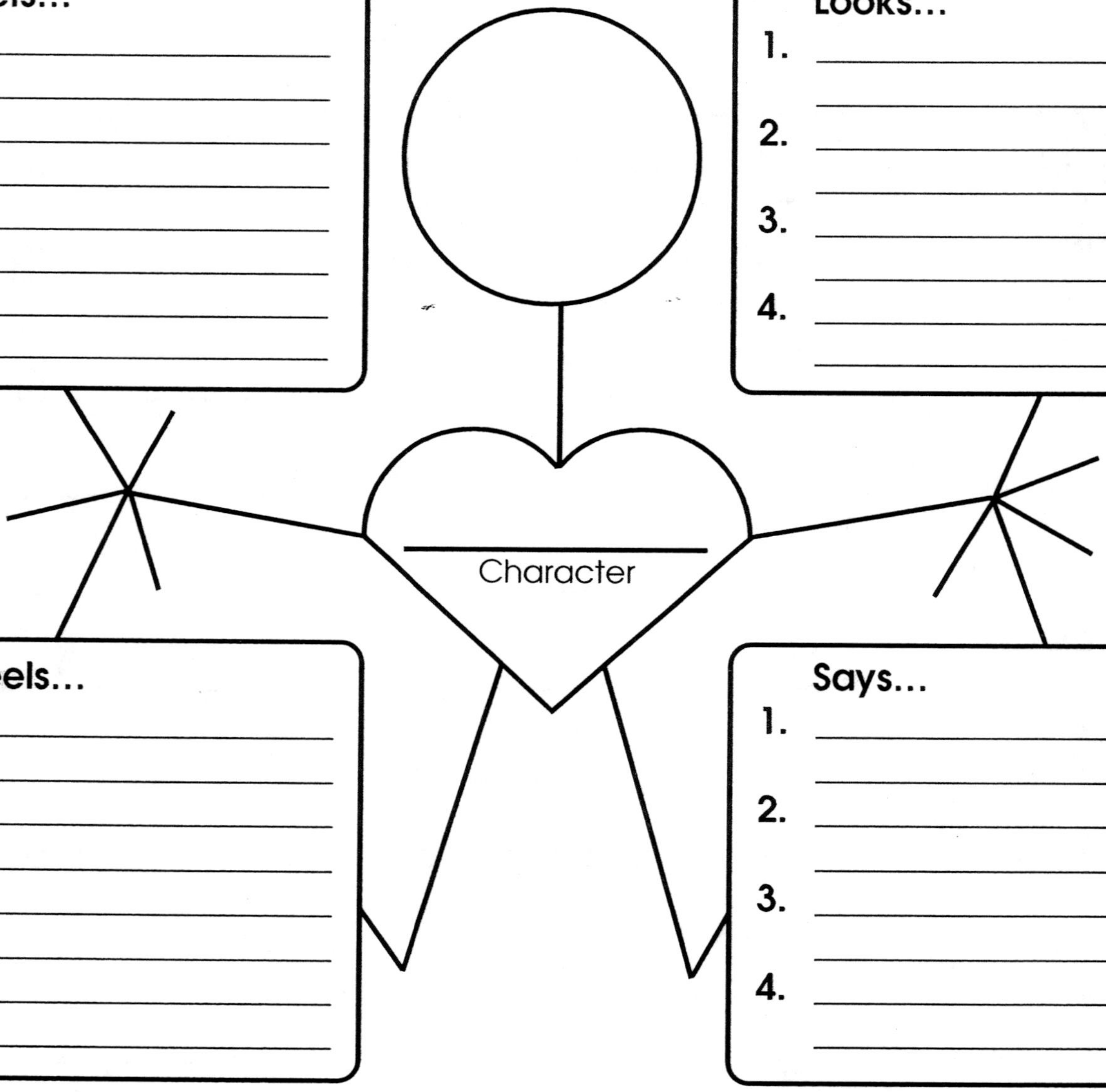

Acts...

1. ____________________
2. ____________________
3. ____________________
4. ____________________

Looks...

1. ____________________
2. ____________________
3. ____________________
4. ____________________

Feels...

1. ____________________
2. ____________________
3. ____________________
4. ____________________

Says...

1. ____________________
2. ____________________
3. ____________________
4. ____________________

Character Analysis #12

Name:	
Date:	
Title:	
Author:	

Create a Puppet

Select a character from your story. Think about how he or she looks. What makes the character interesting?

How to create your puppet:

You will need:

- your book
- a small paper bag
- white construction paper
- a pencil
- colored pencils or crayons
- scissors
- glue

1. **Draw** the character's head, arms, body, clothes, etc. on the construction paper. Remember to include things you find interesting about him or her (for example, a baseball cap for Franklin).
2. **Color** your picture.
3. **Cut** out the head. Then cut out the body and arms. You should have two pieces.
4. **Glue** the head to the bottom flap of the paper bag. Then glue the body below it on the bag.
5. Put on a puppet show for a friend.

Name: ______________________
Date: ______________________
Title: ______________________
Author: ______________________

Book Award

What makes your book exciting and interesting? Does it have great **characters**, **illustrations**, **plot**, or **setting**? Give the book an award for the story element you like the best.

I give this book the Best ______________________ Award.

How to make your book award:

You will need:

- your book
- a small paper plate
- white construction paper
- a pencil
- colored pencils or crayons
- scissors
- glue

1. Write the name of the award on the outer rim of the paper plate, at the top (**example: Best Illustrations Award**).
2. On a small piece of paper, tell why you think the book should get this award. Glue it to the bottom rim of the paper plate.
3. In the center of the plate, draw a picture of why the book deserves this award.
4. Draw two ribbons on construction paper and cut them out. Paste them to the bottom of the plate. On the ribbons, write the book's title, author, illustrator, date, and your name.
5. Color your award.

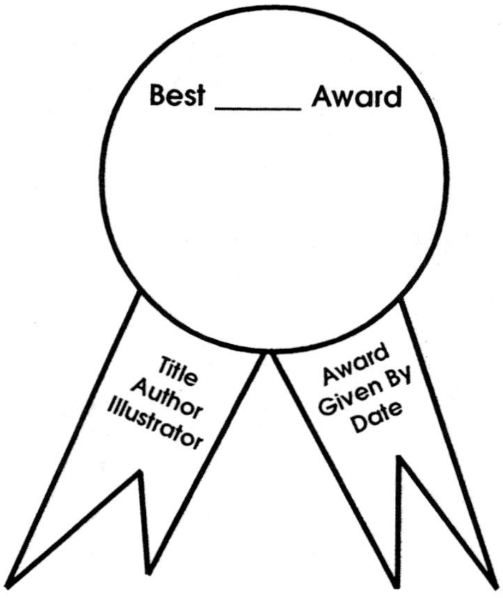

Name: ____________________

Date: ____________________

Title: ____________________

Author: ____________________

Retell Chain

You will need:

- your book
- colored construction paper
- a pencil
- colored pencils or crayons
- scissors
- glue

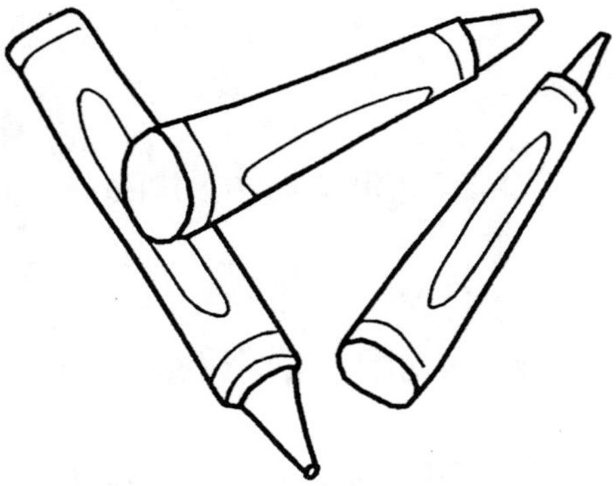

How to create a chain story:

1. Cut construction paper into five 2.5-centimeter (1-inch) strips.
2. Think about the story. How does it start? What happens next? What happens at the end?
3. On each strip, write one event from the story. Use the words **First**, **Then**, **Next**, **After**, and **Finally**.
4. Order your strips in the way the events happen in the story.
5. Glue each strip into a circle. Be sure to join the first event to the next event that occurs in the story to make your retell chain.

Name:	____________
Date:	____________
Title:	____________
Author:	____________

Character Mask

Make a mask of your favorite character from your story. Then put on a play.

You will need:

- your book
- white construction paper
- a pencil
- colored pencils or crayons
- yarn or colored paper
- lined paper
- scissors
- glue

1. **Draw** the shape of the mask on construction paper. Make it big enough to cover your face.
2. **Cut** out the mask.
3. **Color** the mask to look like the character. Use yarn or different colored paper for hair.
4. **Cut** out a small piece of lined paper, small enough to be glued to the back of the mask.
5. **Write** the lines on the paper that the character from your story is to say.
6. **Glue** the paper onto the mask. Be sure that you will be able to read the lines, when the mask is held up to your face.
7. **Tell** the title of your story, and who your character is before you do the play.

For even more fun, get a friend who is reading the same book to perform the play with you.

Name: ____________________

Date: ____________________

Title: ____________________

Author: ____________________

Then What Happened?

Tell what happened at the very **end** of your story. Then write what you think could happen next.

Include:

- What might the characters do or say?
- Where might they go?
- Why would they do these things?
- How would they do them?

At the end of the story ____________________

____

____

After ____________________

____

____

____

____

____

____

____

Creative Thinking Activities #5

Name: ____________________

Date: ____________________

Title: ____________________

Author: ____________________

Design a Cover

Materials you will need:

- a large piece of white construction paper
- a pencil
- colored pencils, markers or crayons
- one piece of lined paper

Design a new book cover for your story. Make it **colorful** and **interesting** so that other people will want to read your book. Think about your favorite part of the story to get some ideas for the cover illustration.

1. Fold the construction paper in half, and then fold both ends of the paper under to make 2.5-centimeter (1-inch) flaps.

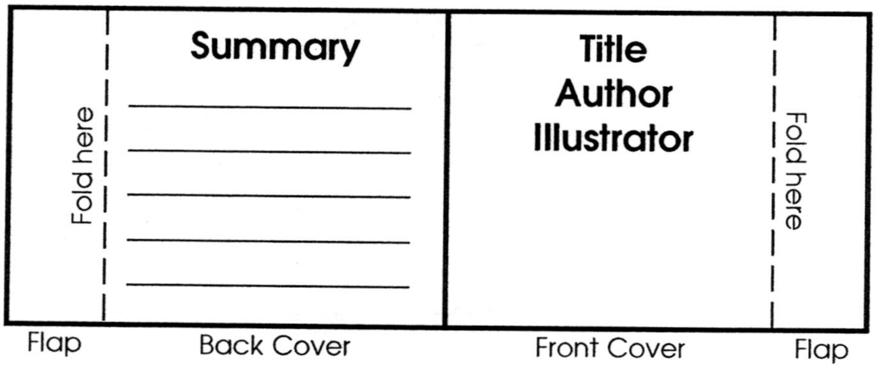

2. Draw an **illustration** on the front cover. Make sure you add the title, author, and illustrator above your picture.

3. Cut the lined paper to fit on the back of the cover. On the paper, write a short **summary** of the story that will tell the reader what the book is about, and get them to read it.

Name:	______________________
Date:	______________________
Title:	______________________
Author:	______________________

Picture Perfect

Art is a beautiful way to show your feelings about a story.

Draw a picture of how you feel about your story. **Color** your picture.

On the back of this page, **tell** how you feel about the story.

Creative Thinking Activities #7

Name: ____________________

Date: ____________________

Title: ____________________

Author: ____________________

Bookmark

Make a keepsake bookmark of your book.

Directions:

- Cut out the bookmark.
- **Draw** a picture of the story; include the title and the author's name.
- **Write** about the event in the picture and why you chose it.
- **Color** your bookmark.
- **Share** it with a friend.

Title: ____________________

Author: ____________________

____

____

____

____

Name: ______________________

Date: ______________________

Title: ______________________

Author: ______________________

Add a Character

Add a new character to your story. **List five** of his or her characteristics on the graphic organizer. **Tell** why this character would improve your story.

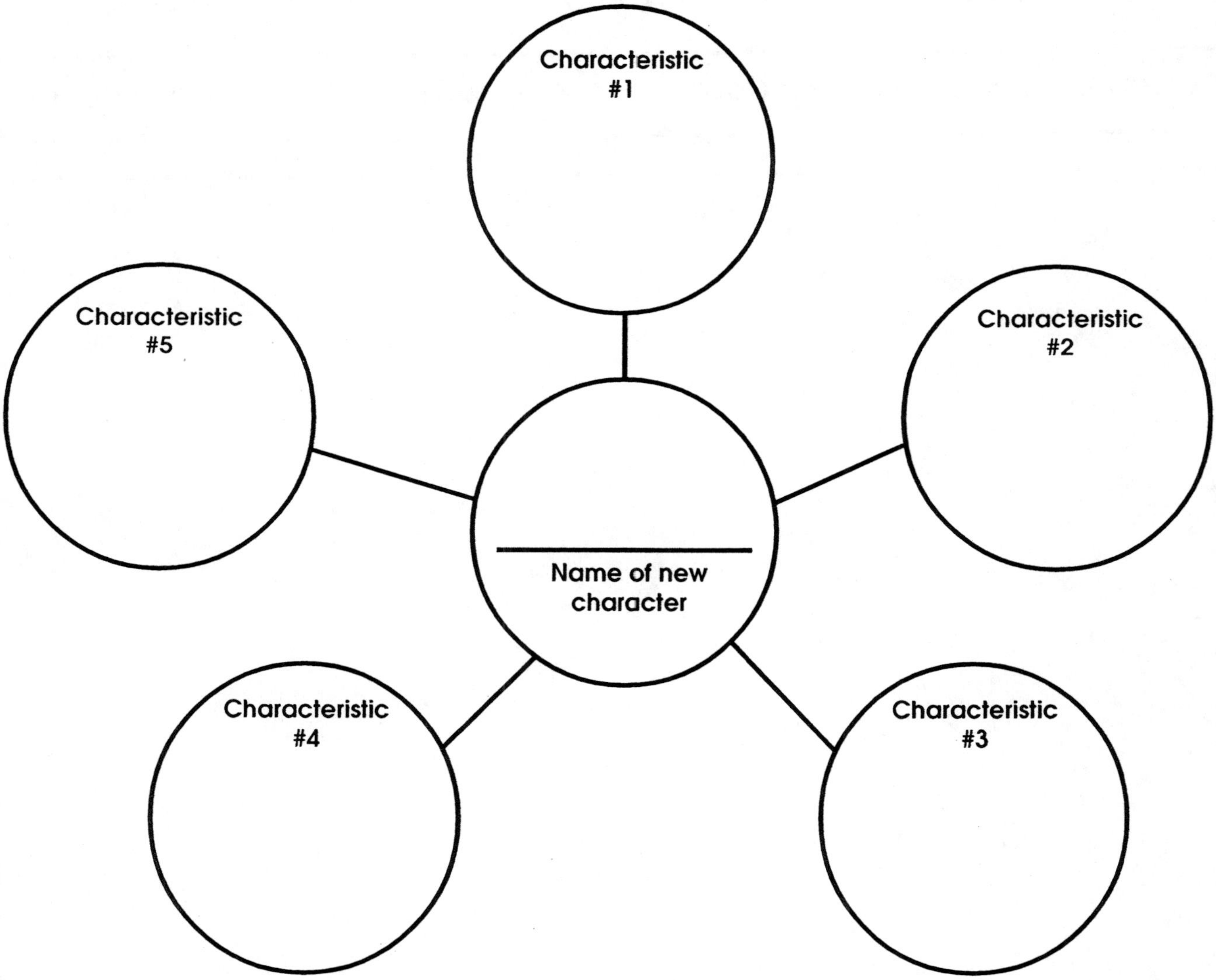

This character would imporve the story because ______________________

____

____

Creative Thinking Activities #9

Name: ______________________
Date: ______________________
Title: ______________________
Author: ______________________

Join the Story

You move next door to the main character in your story. **Draw** a picture of you and the character. Show what you would be doing together.

Example: If you lived next door to Franklin, you might be playing soccer.

Creative Thinking Activities #10

Name:	______________________
Date:	______________________
Title:	______________________
Author:	______________________

Poster Power

Draw a poster that tells about your book. It should be interesting so that other people will want to read the story.

Remember to include the title and author of the book.

Choose one topic from below:

- Your **favorite** part of the book.
- The most **interesting** part of the book.
- Three things you **learned** about the topic of the book.

Present the poster to the class.

Materials you will need:

- **a large piece of white construction paper or Bristol board**
- **a pencil**
- **markers, crayons, colored pencils or paint**

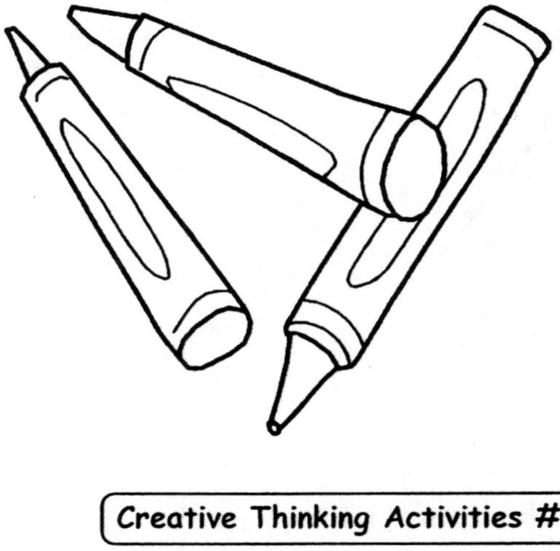

Creative Thinking Activities #11

Name: ______________________

Date: ______________________

Title: ______________________

Author: ______________________

Memory Stone

Make a memory stone of your book. Draw **five** small pictures of the most memorable or interesting parts.

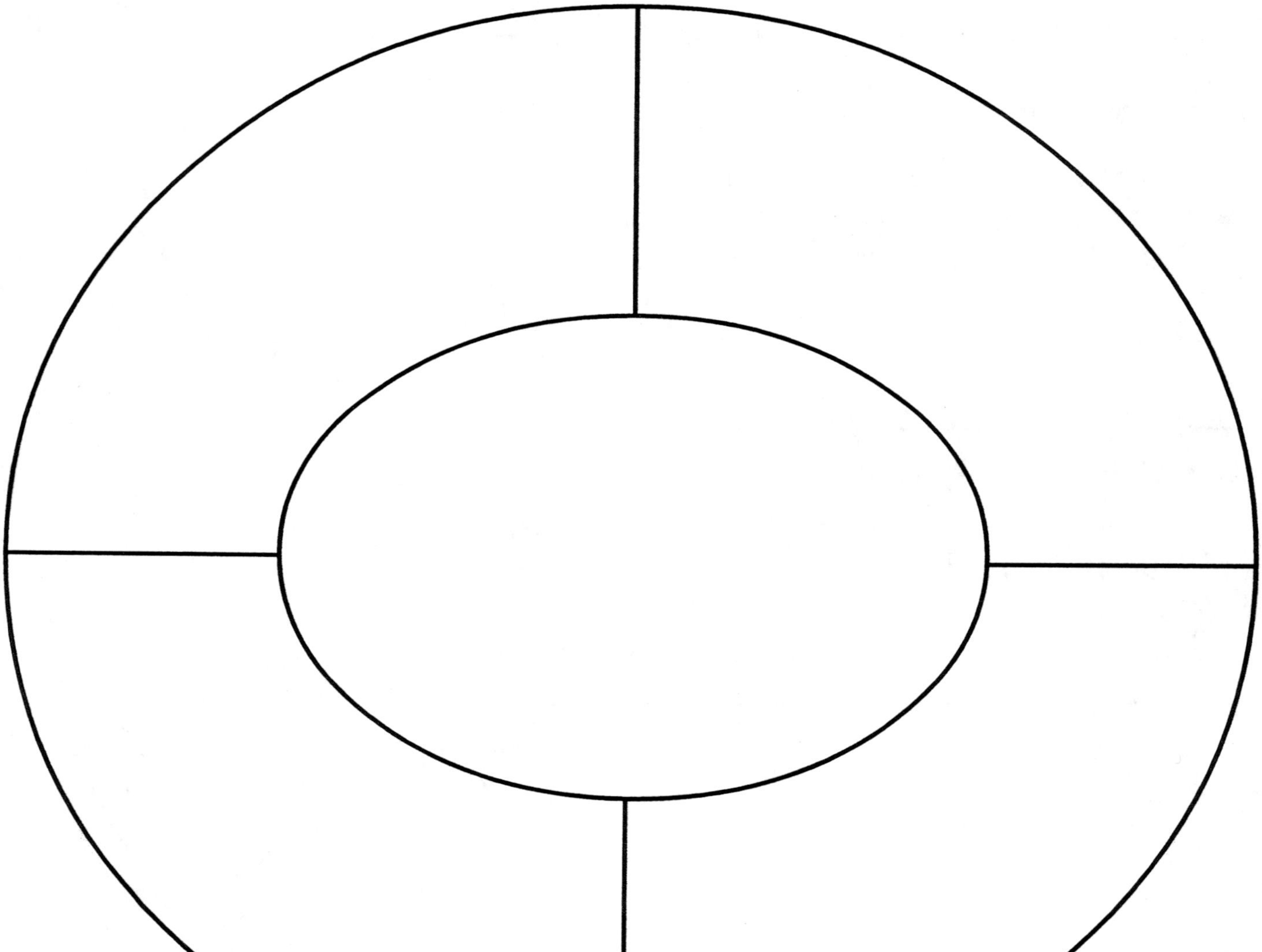

Creative Thinking Activities #12

Name:	____________________
Date:	____________________
Title:	____________________
Author:	____________________

Looking Into Pictures

Look at the pictures in your story. Fill in the chart below by looking at **three** different pictures. In the first column, write what you **see** in the picture. Write what the picture **tells** you in the second column.

In the picture I see ...	The picture tells me ...
1.	
2.	
3.	

Creative Thinking Activities #13

Name: ____________________
Date: ____________________
Title: ____________________
Author: ____________________

Make a Connection

Share your thoughts by answering the questions.

What did you think the book was going to be about **before** reading it?

Example: I thought it was going to be about Franklin and Harriet playing.

____

____

____

What did the story make you **think** of?

Example: The story made me think of the time I fell off the swing.

____

____

____

What do you **wonder** about?

Example: I wonder if Franklin would be sad if Harriet got hurt.

____

____

____

Creative Thinking Activities #14

Name: ______________________

Date: ______________________

Title: ______________________

Author: ______________________

Star Story

Use your book to help you **retell** the story. In each point of the star, **draw** a picture to show what happened in the story. In the center, **draw** a picture of the main character.

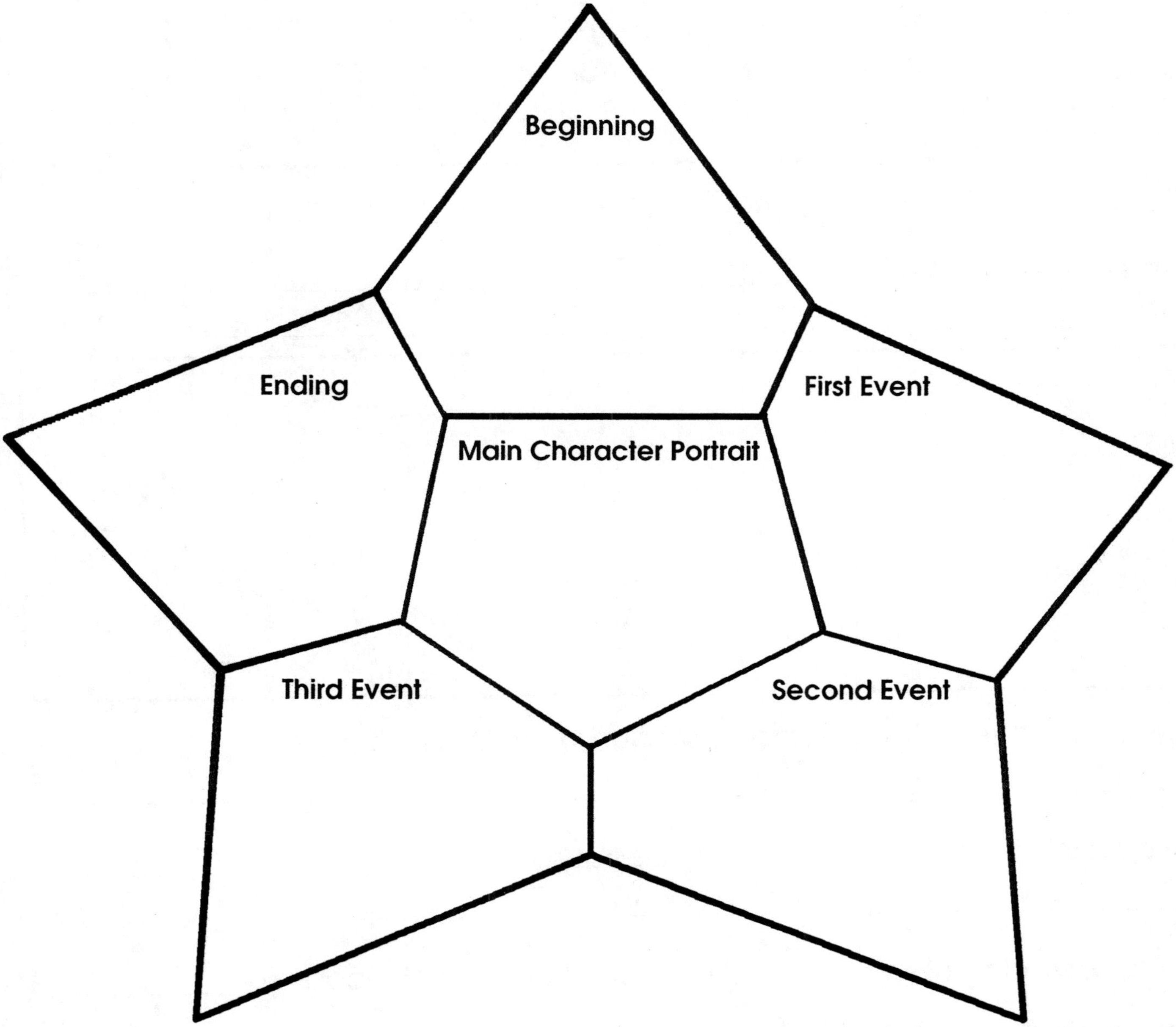

Creative Thinking Activities #15

Name: ______________________
Date: ______________________
Title: ______________________
Author: ______________________

Book Reviewer Report

You are a book reviewer for a magazine. Your job is to report on your book and persuade others to read it or not to read it, by answering the questions below. Use the star scale to rate your book.

☆	☆☆	☆☆☆	☆☆☆☆	☆☆☆☆☆
1	**2**	**3**	**4**	**5**
worst	okay	good	very good	best

This book is: ❒ **fiction** ❒ **nonfiction**

This book is about ____

____

This is a picture of my favorite **illustration** in the book. It is ______________

____

I would **award** this book _____ stars because ______________________

____

I **would/would not** recommend this book to a friend because ______________

____

Synthesis and Evaluation #1

Name: ____________________

Date: ____________________

Title: ____________________

Author: ____________________

Book Talk

Answer the questions and **illustrate** your favorite part of the story. Then **share** your thoughts about the book with a friend.

I chose this book because ____________________

____

____

This book makes me think of ____________________

____

____

My favorite character in the book was ____________________ because ______

____

____

This is a picture of my favorite part of the book. It is ____________________

____

____

Synthesis and Evaluation #2

Name: ____________________
Date: ____________________
Title: ____________________
Author: ____________________

Tell a Friend

Would you recommend this book to a friend? ❐ Yes ❐ No
Why? ____________________

What **three** things would you tell a friend about this book?

1. ____________________
2. ____________________
3. ____________________

If you could change a part of the book, what would you change?

____

How would you change it? ____________________

Synthesis and Evaluation #3

Name: ______________________

Date: ______________________

Title: ______________________

Author: ______________________

Analyzer

Analyze the book by completing the sentences and illustrating the sections.

Beginning

This story begins with ______________________

____

____

Ending

The story ends with ______________________

____

____

I think ______________________

____

____

Synthesis and Evaluation #4

Name: ____________________
Date: ____________________
Title: ____________________
Author: ____________________

Character Critic

Who was the most important character in the book?

____

____

____

Why do you think so?

____

____

____

Which character is most like you? ____________________

Why do you think so?

____

____

____

Which character would you like for a friend? ____________________

Why? ______________________________

____

____

Synthesis and Evaluation #5

Name: ____________________

Date: ____________________

Title: ____________________

Author: ____________________

Problem Solver

Identify the **plot** or **problem** in the book and how it was solved by completing the sentences and illustrating the sections.

The Problem

The problem in the story was ____________________

____

____

The Solution

The solution to the problem was ____________________

____

____

If I was a character in the story, I would have ____________________

____

____

Synthesis and Evaluation #6

Name: ____________________
Date: ____________________
Title: ____________________
Author: ____________________

Climbing Climax

The **climax** is the **highest point of conflict** in the plot, or the turning point before the problem is resolved. Use your book to record **three** events in the triangle that lead up to the climax.

The climax of the story is ____

____

Events leading up to the climax:

Synthesis and Evaluation #7

Name: ________________________
Date: ________________________
Title: ________________________
Author: ________________________

List the Facts

Books are either **fiction** (made up) or **nonfiction** (true or factual). **List** the reasons why you think the book is fiction or nonfiction. Give **specific examples** from your book, and list the **page number** where you found the information.

1. ____

Page ________

2. ____

Page ________

3. ____

Page ________

4. ____

Page ________

5. ____

Page ________

6. ____

Page ________

Synthesis and Evaluation #8

Name: ______________________
Date: ______________________
Title: ______________________
Author: ______________________

Interview an Author

You are a reporter for a magazine. You will be interviewing the author of your book. **Think** about **five** things you want to ask him or her. **Write** them below.

Example: How old were you when you wrote your first book?

1. ______________________

2. ______________________

3. ______________________

4. ______________________

5. ______________________

Synthesis and Evaluation #9

Name: ______________________
Date: ______________________
Title: ______________________
Author: ______________________

Character Chat

With a partner, select a scene from your book that you would like to chat with the character about. Take turns pretending to be the character from the scene and the interviewer, and answer the questions below.

Character ______________________ **Scene page** __________

The interviewer says:

1. Describe your role in the book. ______________________
____

2. What is this scene about? ______________________
____

3. In this scene, why did you ______________________?
____

4. What were you thinking when you did that? ______________________
____

5. How does it feel to be in a book? ______________________
____

6. I think ______________________
____
____

Synthesis and Evaluation #10

Name: ______________________
Date: ______________________
Title: ______________________
Author: ______________________

Book Buddy

Choose a friend to read the book with.

Before you read the book, talk about what you think the book will be about. Write out your prediction.

We predict that the book will be about ______________________

____

As you read, talk about the book: What is happening? What does it remind you of? What do you think might happen next?

Write out the answer to **one** of these questions.

____

____

____

After you have finished reading, talk about your favorite part. What did you each like best about the book? What did it remind you of?

Complete **one** activity:

- Act out a scene from the book.
- Draw a picture about the book.
- Make a poster advertising the book so others will want to read it.

Synthesis and Evaluation #11

Name: ______________________
Date: ______________________
Title: ______________________
Author: ______________________

It All Changed

Start from where your story ended. How can you make it different? Change the story by writing your own ending.

Example: The giant caught Jack and took him back to his castle. He was lonely and wanted a friend. They lived happily ever after together in the sky. Jack was never hungry again.

At the end of the story ____

Synthesis and Evaluation #12

Literature Response Forms

Literature Response Forms

Literature Response Forms

Literature Response Forms